WHAT CHRISTIANS BELIEVE

WHAT CHRISTIANS BELIEVE

MOODY PUBLISHERS • CHICAGO

ISBN: 978-0-8024-1195-2

We hope you enjoy this book from Moody Publishers. Our goal is to provide high-quality, thought-provoking books and products that connect truth to your real needs and challenges. For more information on other books and products written and produced from a biblical perspective, go to www.moodypublishers.com or write to:

Moody Publishers
820 N. LaSalle Boulevard
Chicago, IL 60610

1 3 5 7 9 10 8 6 4 2

Printed in the United States of America

These studies were prepared by the following staff members of the Emmaus Bible School:

Alfred P. Gibbs	Harold Shaw
R. Edward Harlow	Dudley A. Sherwood
Harold M. Harper	John Smart
George M. Landis	C. Ernest Tatham
Harold G. Mackay	Ben Tuininga

William McDonald

CONTENTS

WHAT CHRISTIANS BELIEVE

Chapter 1

THE BIBLE

I. INTRODUCTION

SOMEONE has called the Holy Bible "the divine library," and this is a true statement. Although we think of the Bible as one book, yet it is made up of sixty-six separate books.

These books, beginning with Genesis and ending with Revelation, are divided into two main sections. The first section is called the Old Testament and contains thirty-nine books. The second section is the New Testament and it has twenty-seven books.

At the beginning of each Bible is an index which lists the names of the books, and tells the page number on which each book begins.

II. WHO WROTE THE BIBLE?

From the human standpoint the Bible was written by not less than thirty-six authors over a period of about sixteen hundred years. But the important thing to remember is that these men wrote under the direct control of God. God guided them in writing the very words. This is what we mean by inspiration. The following Scriptures clearly teach that the Bible is inspired by God.

> For the prophecy came not in old time by the will of man, but holy men of God spake as they were moved by the Holy Ghost. 2 Peter 1:21.
>
> All Scripture is given by inspiration of God and is profitable for doctrine, for reproof, for correction, for instruction in righteousness; that the man of God may be perfect, throughly furnished unto all good works. 2 Timothy 3:16-17.

Thus the Bible *is* the Word of God. It is not enough to say that the Bible *contains* the Word of God. This might imply that parts of it are inspired and parts are not. *Every part of the Bible is inspired.* "All Scripture is given by inspiration of God."

Another important point to remember is that the Bible is the *only* written revelation which God has given to man. In the last chapter of the Bible, God warns men against adding to the Bible or taking away from it. Revelation 22:18-19.

III. WHAT IS THE SUBJECT OF THE BIBLE?

Although the Bible is made up of sixty-six books, yet it has one main subject. Christ is the grand theme of Scripture. The Old Testament contains many predictions, or prophecies, concerning Christ. The New Testament tells of His coming.

IV. WHAT DOES THE BIBLE CONTAIN?

The Bible is the record of the world from the beginning of time until the future when there will be a new heaven and a new earth.

Genesis tells of the creation of the world, the entrance of sin, the flood, and the beginning of the nation of Israel. From Exodus to Esther we have the history of Israel up to about 400 years before the birth of Christ. The books from Job to the Song of Solomon contain wonderful poetry and wisdom. The rest of the Old Testament, from Isaiah to Malachi, is prophetic, — that is, these books contain messages from God to Israel concerning its present condition and its future destiny.

The New Testament opens with four Gospels, each of which presents the life of the Lord Jesus Christ. Acts tells the story of the Christian movement in its infancy and the life of the great apostle Paul. From Romans to Jude, we find letters to churches and individuals, concerning the great truths of the Christian faith, and practical instruction concerning the Christian life. Revelation gives us a glimpse into the future,—to events that will yet take place in heaven, on earth, and in hell.

V. CONCLUSION

"This book contains the mind of God, the state of man, the way of salvation, the doom of sinners and the happiness of believers. Its doctrines are holy, its precepts are binding, its histories are true, and its decisions are immutable. Read it to be wise, believe it to be saved, and practice it to be holy. It contains light to direct you, food to support you, and comfort to cheer you. It is the traveler's map, the pilot's compass, the soldier's sword, and the Christian's charter. Here Paradise is restored, Heaven opened, and the gates of Hell disclosed. Christ is its grand subject, our good its design, and the glory of God its end. Read it slowly, frequently, prayerfully. It is a mine of wealth, a paradise of glory, and a river of pleasure. It will reward the greatest labor, and condemn all who trifle with its sacred contents. It is the Book of Books—God's Book—the revelation of God to man." Selected.

Chapter 2

GOD

NO GREATER SUBJECT can occupy the mind than the study of God and of man's relationship to Him.

I. THE EXISTENCE OF GOD

1. The Bible does not seek to prove the existence of God. The fact that there is a God is assumed throughout the Scriptures. The first verse of the Bible is an example. "In the beginning God created the heaven and the earth." God's existence is presented as a statement of fact that needs no proof. The man who says that there is no God is called a fool in Psalm 14:1.

2. However, even apart from the Bible, there are certain evidences for the existence of God. (1) Mankind has always believed in a universal being. (2) Creation must have a creator. The

universe could not originate without a cause. (3) The wonderful design which we see in creation demands an infinite designer. (4) Since man is an intelligent, moral being, his creator must have been of a much higher order in order to create him.

II. THE NATURE OF GOD

1. God is a spirit. (John 4:24). This means that God does not have a body. He is invisible. However, He can reveal Himself to man in visible form. In the person of Jesus Christ, God came into the world in a body of flesh. John 1:14, 18; Colossians 1:15; Hebrews 1:3.

2. God is a person. Personal names are used in reference to Him. Exodus 3:14. Matthew 11:25. Personal characteristics are ascribed to Him, such as (1) knowledge, Isaiah 55:9-10; (2) emotions, Genesis 6:6; and (3) will, Joshua 3:10.

3. The Unity of God. Scripture clearly teaches that there is one God. I Timothy 2:5 (Read this verse.) The false teaching that there are many gods is contrary to reason. There can be only one Supreme Being.

4. The Trinity. The Bible teaches not only that there is one God, but also that there are three persons in the Godhead,—Father, Son and Holy

Spirit. This is a mystery to the human mind, but although it cannot be understood, it can be believed because God's Word says it is so. The word "trinity" is not found in the Bible, but the truth is found in the following passages.

(1) Baptism of Jesus, Matthew 3:16-17.

(2) The great commission, Matthew 28:19.

(3) The benediction of II Corinthians 13:14.

The Father is called God in Romans 1:7. The Son is called God in Hebrews 1:8. The Holy Spirit is called God in Acts 5:3-4.

III. THE ATTRIBUTES OF GOD

It is difficult to define God. One of the best ways is to describe certain of His qualities or characteristics. These are known as His attributes.

1. God is omnipresent. This means that God is present everywhere at the same time. Jeremiah 23:24.

2. God is omniscient. In other words, He knows all things. He knows every thought and deed of man. Proverbs 15:3. He knows everything that takes place in nature, including even the death of a sparrow, Matthew 10:29.

"Though limitless the universe, and gloriously
grand,

He knows the eternal story of every grain of sand."

3. God is omnipotent. He has all power. He created the universe, and now controls it by His power. There is nothing that He cannot do. Matthew 19:26.

4. God is eternal. He never had a beginning, and He will never cease to exist. Psalm 90:2.

5. God is unchangeable. "I am the Lord, I change not." Malachi 3:6.

6. God is holy. He is absolutely pure and sinless. He hates sin and loves goodness. Proverbs 15:9, 26. He must separate Himself from sinners, and must punish sin. Isaiah 59:1, 2.

7. God is just. Everything He does is right and fair. He fulfills all His promises. Psalm 119:137.

8. God is love. Although God hates sin, yet He loves sinners. John 3:16 (Read this verse.)

Note: In speaking to God in prayer, we use the words "Thou" and "Thee." The purpose of this is to show reverence for God. It is not proper to address Him in the same way that we would speak to our fellow-men.

Chapter 3

MAN

If we want to know the truth about man, we must turn to the Bible. "Truth is what God says about a thing." The Bible tells us about man's creation, nature, relation to other beings, his fall and destiny.

I. MAN'S ORIGIN

It is only natural that man should be curious about his origin. He always has been. Various theories have been put forward at different times by philosophers. The most modern is the theory of evolution, which asserts that man's ancestors are the lower animals.

But the Bible tells us: In the beginning God created the heavens and the earth . . . God created man. Gen. 1:1, 27.

God says concerning His creature man, "I have created him for my glory, I have formed him: yea, I have made him." (Isaiah 43:7). So the old question, "What is the chief end of man?" is properly answered, "The chief end of man is to glorify God."

II. MAN'S NATURE

Anyone who has witnessed a deathbed understands vividly that man has a physical body and also a soul or spirit. At one moment the person is alive . . . the next he is gone. Yet his body is still there. But the life principle has departed; a dead body remains. Man is not merely a body, but also is or has a soul and spirit.

The Bible teaches us that man exists as a threefold being: body, soul and spirit (I Thessalonians 5:23). While it is hard for us to distinguish between soul and spirit, since both are in contrast with the physical body, the Bible shows that there is a difference. Animals have a body and soul, but no spirit. A man has body, soul and spirit.

The soul distinguishes a living being from a dead one, but the spirit distinguishes a man from an animal. The spirit of man makes it possible for him to have communion or fellowship with God.

The soul is the seat of the emotions and passions, while the term spirit includes our ability to know and reason. Man is responsible to God and it is his greatest duty to find out what God wants him to do, then do it.

III. MAN'S FREE WILL

There are other beings in the universe which God has created. These are angels or spirits. They do not have human body or soul. They are mightier than we are. They were also created to serve God, but since they have a free will, some of them fell into the sin of disobedience.

God could have made a number of machines to do His will mechanically. Instead He chose to create beings who could, if they wished, serve Him voluntarily and love Him freely. We can quite understand why He would desire to have it so. A man could get protection for his house by means of a burglar alarm system. But there is something about a dog which draws out our affections in a way no machine ever could.

IV. MAN'S SIN

When God created free beings, able to do His

will or refuse to do so, He must have known that some would choose the wrong way. And so it turned out. A great angel called Lucifer, now known as Satan, decided to set his will in opposition to God's. He was immediately cast out of heaven, and many other angels were cast out with him. From that time on, Satan has sought to hinder the plans of God in every possible way. When man was created with a free will, Satan immediately planned to tempt him from the path of obedience. God had warned man, but Satan succeeded only too well in drawing him into sin as well. The well-known story is found in Genesis 3.

Now God, as the moral Governor of the universe, cannot tolerate in His presence any being who deliberately disobeys His commands. This is why Satan was cast out of heaven when he defied God's will. The same treatment was necessary for man, and so Adam was driven from the presence of God.

Adam's nature has been passed on to every member of the human race. We are all born—with a tendency to sin. This nature responds to temptation from without and so we yield and grievously sin.

V. MAN'S FUTURE

Just as the Bible tells us of man's origin, as coming from the hand of God; and of man's shameful fall and the consequent separation from God; so it faithfully tells us that every man, woman and child will some day stand before God as his Judge. The fact of death is so common that everyone understands the inevitable end of every man. But the Bible adds, "After this the judgment." God has created man and revealed to him His will. God will absolutely hold every person responsible for everything he has done. This life is primarily a preparation for the next one. Man does not die like the animal. His spirit must go to God, his Creator and Judge.

Chapter 4

SIN

I. WHAT IS SIN?

No one can read the Bible very much without realizing that a great deal of attention is given to the subject of sin, its cause and cure. We often think of sin in connection with crime and murder. But sin in the Bible refers to anything short of God's perfection. In Romans 3:23, we read, "All have sinned and come short of the glory of God." The "glory of God" includes the thought of absolute perfection. Sin is therefore falling short of the mark. All men are guilty of this.

Sin is also spoken of in the Bible in the following ways.

1. Breaking the law of God. Romans 5:13.
2. Rebellion against God, or lawlessness. I John 3:4 (Revised Version).
3. Moral impurity. Psalm 32:5.

Evil thoughts are sinful, as well as evil deeds. Matthew 5:28.

II. THE ORIGIN OF SIN

The first recorded instance of sin took place in heaven. The angel Lucifer became ambitious to be equal with God. Isaiah 14:12-14. For this sin of pride, he was cast out of heaven, and became the one whom the Bible elsewhere describes as the devil or Satan.

The first instance of sin on earth is described in the Third Capter of Genesis. It took place in the Garden of Eden. God forbade Adam and Eve to eat the fruit of the tree of the knowledge of good and evil. They disobeyed God and ate the forbidden fruit. They thus became sinners.

III. THE RESULTS OF SIN

1. As soon as the parents of the human race sinned, they became conscious of the fact that they were naked, and they tried to hide from God. Genesis 3:10.

2. The penalty of sin is death. Adam became spiritually dead the moment he sinned. By this we mean that he became separated from God, and banished from God's presence. He also became subject to physical death. Although he did not die im-

mediately, his body was doomed to die eventually.

3. Adams' sinful nature was passed on to all the human race. Every child born of sinful parents is a sinner by birth. Thus Adam's oldest son, Cain, was a murderer. Because all men are born sinners, they are all dead spiritually, and are all doomed to die physically some day. (Read Romans 5:12-18 carefully at this point.)

4. Man's sin brought God's curse upon all creation. Thorns and thistles, for instance, are an evidence of this. Other evidences are mentioned in Genesis 3:14-19. Sin needs no proof as long as we have prisons, hospitals, and funeral parlors. Tears, sickness, sorrow, pain and death are some of the results of sin.

IV. THE PENALTY OF SIN

"The wages of sin is death." Romans 6:23. God has pronounced the penalty of sin as being death. We have already seen that this means spiritual death and physical death. This penalty must be paid. God must punish sin.

As long as a man lives in his sins, he is dead spiritually and is facing physical death. If he is still in his sins when he dies, he is subject to eternal death. This means that he will be forever banished from God and will suffer for his sins in the lake of fire. This is the second death spoken of in Revelation 20:14.

V. THE REMEDY FOR SIN

God has provided a remedy so that men do not need to suffer everlasting punishment for their sins. He sent His Son into the world to provide a way of escape for man. The Lord Jesus Christ was born of the Virgin Mary. He did not inherit Adam's sinful nature. He was the only sinless man who ever lived. On the Cross of Calvary He willingly suffered the penalty of sin, and satisfied all God's holy demands. Since the penalty of sin has been met, God can now give eternal life to every sinner who confesses the fact that he is a sinner and receives the Lord Jesus Christ as his Lord and Savior. (This will be more fully explained in the lesssons on the New Birth and Salvation.)

When a person trusts in Christ, he is saved from the penalty and power of sin. This does not mean that he no longer commits sin. But it does mean that all his sins, past, present and future, have been forgiven, that he will never be judged for them, and that he has power to live for God instead of for the pleasures of sin.

Chapter 5

CHRIST

THIS LESSON concerns the Lord Jesus Christ—the central theme of Holy Scripture. We shall consider His deity, His incarnation, His work and His offices.

I. HIS DEITY

The deity of Christ means that Christ is God. Scripture clearly teaches this important fact in the following ways.

1. The attributes of God are used in speaking of Christ.

a. His pre-existence. Christ has no beginning. John 17:5.

b. His omnipresence. He is with His servants everywhere. Matthew 28:20.

c. His omnipotence. He has unlimited power. Revelation 1:18.

d. His omniscience. He has unlimited knowledge. John 21:17.

e. His unchangeableness. He is "the same, yesterday, today and forever." Hebrews 13:8.

2. The works of God were performed by Christ.

a. He created all things. John 1:3.

b. He upholds the universe. Colossians 1:16.

c. He raised Himself from the dead. John 2:19.

3. The titles of God are given to Christ.

a. God the Father addresses the Son as God. Hebrews 1:8.

b. Men called Him God, and He did not refuse their worship. John 20:28.

c. Demons recognized Him as God. Mark 1:24.

d. He declared Himself to be God. John 10:30.

II. HIS INCARNATION

By the incarnation of Christ is meant His coming into the world as a man.

1. The coming of Christ was predicted in the Old Testament. Isaiah 7:14.

2. History records the birth of our Lord. His birth was different from all other births.

a. He was conceived by the Holy Ghost. Luke 1:35.

b. He was born of a virgin. Matthew 1:23.

c. Yet He was truly man, possessing a body (Hebrews 10:5), soul (Matthew 26:38) and spirit (Luke 23:46).

3. Christ came in human form in order to:

a. Reveal the Father. John 14:9.

b. Put away sin by the sacrifice of Himself. Hebrews 9:26.

c. Destroy the works of the devil. I John 3:8.

NOTE WELL: One of the foundation truths of the Christian faith is that Jesus Christ is truly God and that He came into the world as a man by the miracle of virgin birth. As a man, He was absolutely sinless.

III. HIS WORK

Under this heading, we shall discuss the Lord's death, resurrection and ascension.

1. His death.

a. The death of Christ was necessary. John 3:14.

It was part of God's eternal purpose. Hebrews 10:7.

It was necessary to fulfill Old Testament prophecies. Isaiah 53:5.
It was necessary to provide salvation for man. Ephesians 1:7.

b. The death of Christ was for others. He died as a substitute. I Corinthians 15:3.

c. The death of Christ was sufficient. It completely meets God's claims because Christ endured and exhausted the judgment of God against sin. It completely meets man's need because it was the death of an Infinite Person, and therefore its value is infinite.

2. His resurrection.

a. The resurrection of Christ was necessary to fulfill prophecy, to complete the work of the Cross, Romans 4:25, and to enable Christ to undertake His present work in heaven..

b. Christ's resurrected body was real. It was not a spirit. Luke 24:39. It was the same body which was crucified because it had the print of the nails and the spearwound. John 20:27. Yet it was a changed body, with power to overcome physical limitations.

c. After His resurrection, Christ appeared to certain of His followers at least ten times. More than five hundred reliable witnesses saw

Him after He arose. I Corinthians 15:6.

d. The resurrection of Christ is an important truth. If there had been no resurrection, there would be no Christian faith.

3. His ascension.

a. At the end of His ministry on earth, Christ was carried up into heaven. Mark 16:19. Acts 1:9.

b. He ascended so that He might enter into His reward, John 17:5, and continue His ministry for His people.

IV. HIS OFFICES

Christ is presented in Scripture as a Prophet, a Priest and a King.

1. As Prophet, He tells men what God has to say to them, and He thus reveals God to men. John 1:18.

2. As Priest, He represents believers before God. Hebrews 4:14-16.

3. As King, He reigns today in the hearts of those who are loyal to Him. In a coming day, He will reign upon the earth for one thousand years. Psalm 72 describes His reign on earth.

Then throughout eternity the Lord Jesus will continue to serve His blood-bought people.

Chapter 6

THE NEW BIRTH

John 3:1-21

INTRODUCTION

THE READER must be struck by the fact that the Lord Jesus Christ, the Son of God, solemnly impressed upon a most religious and moral person named Nicodemus the absolute necessity for him to be born again, if he would see or enter the Kingdom of God (vs. 3, 5). The new birth is one of the three great "*musts*" of all humanity. 1. The "must" of *death* (II Samuel 14:14; Hebrews 9: 27). 2. The "must" of the *judgment* (Romans 14:12; Revelation 20:11-15). 3. The "must" of *regeneration,* or the new birth.

In view of much ignorance and misunderstanding concerning this vital matter, let us first view it negatively.

I. WHAT THE NEW BIRTH IS NOT.
(See John 1:12, 13)

1. *It is not of natural generation* or descent—"not of blood." Though one may be born of Christian parents this does not constitute him a Christian.

2. *Not of self-determination*—"will of the flesh." Just as a child cannot will itself to be born physically, so no one can produce the new birth by his own efforts.

3. *Not of human mediation*—"nor of the will of man, but of God." No human being, however eminent his ecclesiastical position, can impart the new birth to another. All the rites and ceremonies of any or of all organized religions can never produce the new birth.

4. *Not a physical change.* Christ corrected Nicodemus' misunderstanding as to this, and showed him it was a spiritual change (vs. 4-6).

5. *Not a social and geographical change.* The born again person is not suddenly translated to heaven, but continues to live on earth, but now to please his Lord and Saviour. (I Corinthians 7:20-24; Colossians 3:22-24).

6. *Not an intellectual apprehension of what it is.* A person can be religiously educated, ordained

to the ministry, and become a preacher without being born again. There are many such. *Theoretically* they may know its necessity, yet know nothing of it by experience.

7. *Not an evolutionary process.* It is not a gradual development of some germ of spiritual life that is within (Ephesians 2:2). Sinners are described as being spiritually *dead.* Life cannot be *developed* where it does not exist!

8. *Not a reformation* or self-improvement by which outwardly bad habits are relinquished. It is not a change of *manners,* but of the *man.*

9. *Not a religious belief.* It is possible to be sincere in one's religious convictions, be baptized, confirmed, join the church, take communion, teach a Sunday School class, occupy a church office, and even be a preacher, without being born again. The necessity for the new birth was stated to one of the most religious, sincere and moral men of his day. (John 3:1.)

10. *The new birth is a spiritual change* (v. 8). This can be brought about only by God (John 1:13).

Now let us ask three questions regarding the new birth. Why? How? When? The first one is discussed below. The other two will be taken up in the next lesson.

II. WHY MUST A PERSON BE BORN AGAIN?

Note verse 7, "Marvel not." The necessity for the new birth is perfectly logical and reasonable, and should not awaken incredulity.

1. *Because of a spiritual nature that man naturally lacks (v. 6).* Here the word "flesh" refers to that sinful nature which a person receives at his physical birth. Leave off the letter "H," and spell it backwards and its meaning will be seen, i.e. "self." Through his sin, Adam acquired a sinful nature, and this nature has been transmitted, by birth, to each of his descendants. (See Romans 5:12, 18, 19; Psalm 51:5.) The *character* of this sinful nature, called "the flesh," is described in Romans 8:5-8. It is "enmity against God, not subject [or obedient] to the law of God," and consequently is incapable of pleasing God. In other words, man does not naturally possess a spiritual capacity which would enable him to either desire, understand, or enjoy the things of God. (See I Corinthians 2:14.)

Just as a musical, artistic or poetic capacity can be communicated to a person only by a *physical* birth, so a spiritual capacity, by which the things of God can be appreciated, must be communicated to a person by a spiritual birth. The flesh can be educated, cultivated and religionized; but its nature remains unchanged and unchangeable in its enmity to God, and is incapable of pleasing God. The new birth is the impartation of a spiritual or Divine nature, by which alone man can possess this spiritual capacity to understand and enjoy the things of God. "That which is born of the flesh is flesh." Like can produce only like!

2. *Because of a spiritual kingdom that man cannot naturally see or enter.* (See vs. 3, 5.) What is meant here by "the Kingdom of God?" It is described as a *spiritual* experience. We read, "The Kingdom of God is not meat and drink [or physical], but righteousness and peace and joy in the Holy Spirit." (Romans 14:17.) Let us think of two kingdoms or spheres; one called "the kingdom of men," and the other "the Kingdom of God"; or one called "the flesh," and the other "the spirit." All humanity enters the kingdom of men by a *physical birth,* which communicates to him a *physical nature,* which fits him for a *physical sphere,* peopled by men. In this sphere he lives, moves, and has his being. Now how is man to be enabled to see the value of and enter this other sphere called the Kingdom of God? The answer is surely

quite obvious. He must be born again, or have a *spiritual* birth, which will introduce him into this new realm. Through this new birth he will become possessed of a *spiritual nature* which will fit him to enjoy the spiritual realities that characterize the Kingdom of God.

You will notice that the marginal rendering of the words "born again," is "born from above." This serves to indicate the source of the birth. Physical birth is of *man* and the *earth;* spiritual birth has its origin in *God* and is from *heaven.* Now read Romans 8:9. Here Paul speaks to a people who were no longer "in the flesh" as to their position before God; but were "in the Spirit." How were they translated from one kingdom to the other? By the Spirit of God, upon their acceptance of Christ as their Savior.

3. *Because of a spiritual life man does not naturally possess.* Man, by nature, is described as being "dead in his trespasses and sins"; "alienated from the life of God"; as "having not life." (See Ephesians 2:1; 4:18; I John 5:11-12.) Just as a body without *physical* life is declared to be physically dead, so any person without *spiritual* life is described in the Bible as being spiritually dead. (See I Timothy 5:6; Luke 15:24.) Death there-

fore means separation. For a person to be separated from Christ, in Whom is life, is to be dead spiritually. (John 1:4.) How can this spiritual life be imparted to the spiritually dead? Let Christ Himself answer it. Turn to John 5:25 and the problem is solved. All who hear the Son of God, receive His Word and trust Him as their Savior receive spiritual life, or are thus born again. See also John 3:16; 5:24; 6:47; 10:26-28; I John 5:13.

Chapter 7

THE NEW BIRTH (Cont'd)

I. HOW CAN A PERSON BE BORN AGAIN?

CHRIST INDICATES a three-fold means by which the new birth is produced.

1. *By believing the Word of God.* John 3:5. The "water" here is the well-known symbol for the Word of God. (See Ephesians 5:26; John 15:3; Psalm 119:9.) It has *no reference to baptism.* Other Scriptures make abundantly clear that the new birth comes through the Word of God. (See I Peter 1:23-25; James 1:18.) Just as water when applied cleanses from our eyes the dirt that would otherwise obscure our vision, so the Word of God, when read and believed, washes from the mind of the sinner his wrong ideas of God and His salvation. The entrance of God's word brings light on man's lost condition (Romans 3:10-19); God's

love as seen in His provision for man's salvation (John 3:16); and the way by which a sinner may be saved (Romans 10:1-17).

2. *By the indwelling of the Spirit of God.* John 3:5. The Holy Spirit, the third Person in the Trinity, was sent by Christ, on His ascension, to use the Word of God to convince men of their sin; to lead them to put their trust in Christ; to indwell each person on believing; to communicate to the believer a Divine nature, or capacity for spiritual things; and to guide each born-again person into all truth. See John 16:7-15; Ephesians 1:13; 4:30; II Peter 1:3, 4; Galatians 5:22-26.

As the Word of God is read or heard, the Holy Spirit applies the truth to the heart in convicting force, showing the sinner his lost, guilty, helpless and hopeless condition. He then reveals through the Word the way of salvation through faith in Christ and His finished work. The moment the sinner trusts in Christ He seals him, by His indwelling presence, as Christ's purchased possession. This is not a question of *feeling,* but of *fact.* We do not feel the new birth.

3. *By faith in the Substitutionary Sacrifice of Christ.* See John 3:14-16. In these words Christ made crystal clear how this new life can come to

a sinner. In answer to Nicodemus' question "How can these things be?" Christ used an incident recorded in the Old Testament to illustrate how the new birth could be experienced. Now read Numbers 21:4-9. Seven words seem to sum up the incident. Let us give it our closest and most careful attention, for it is *Christ's own illustration* of how the sinner can be born again.

a. *Sin* Numbers 21:5. Just as Israel sinned, so all humanity has sinned against God in thought, word and deed. Romans 3:23.

b. *Judgment* v. 6. As their sin brought God's merited judgment upon them, so God has revealed His wrath against all sin. See Romans 1:18; Job 36:18; Romans 6:23.

c. *Repentance* v. 7. Israel realized, confessed, and sought pardon for their sin. This is repentance, which consists of a change of mind, resulting in a change of attitude, which is expressed by a change of action. God demands the repentance of the sinner. See Luke 13:3; Acts 17:31; 20:21; Mark 1:15.

d. *Revelation* v. 8. "And the Lord said"; as God revealed to Moses the way of salvation for these snake-bitten Israelites, so God has revealed in the Bible His way of salvation for us. II Timothy 3:15-17; Romans 10:8-9.

e. *Provision* vs. 8, 9. A serpent of brass was made and lifted up on a pole in full view of the camp of Israel. Now compare John 3:14. Just as Moses lifted up the brazen serpent, so Christ must be lifted up on a cross to provide salvation for sin-bitten humanity. On the cross He bore our sins, took our place, endured all the judgment due to our sins, and by His death, satisfied all God's demands against the sinner. God has indicated His acceptance of the substitutionary sacrifice of His Son by raising Him from the dead. See Isaiah 53: 5, 6; I Corinthians 15:1-4; Romans 5:7-8.

f. *Condition* v. 8—"when he looketh." The fact that the brazen serpent was lifted up did not, of itself, save them. Each bitten Israelite must *look* to *live!* The fact that Christ has died for our sins and accomplished all the work needed for our salvation, will not save any sinner *unless he personally believes on Christ,* trusts Him as his own Savior, and owns Him as the Lord of his life. This is what our Savior meant when He said: "that whosoever *believeth* in him . . . should have everlasting life." John 3:16. Just as the bitten Israelites were not asked to pray, resolve, pay or do good works to merit salvation, so sinners are urged to own their need and trust wholly in the work of Christ, and receive Him by faith as their own personal Savior. See John 1:12; Acts 13:38-39; Ephesians 2:8-9.

g. *Result* v. 9. "he lived." The moment a bitten Israelite (who was as good as dead) looked, he received new life. He was, as it were, born again! So the moment a guilty, lost sinner believes the gospel that Christ died for his sins, and definitely accepts Him as his own Savior, he receives spiritual or eternal life, is indwelt by the Holy Spirit, becomes a partaker of a Divine nature, and is thus born from above, or regenerated. This is the new birth, which Christ declared was absolutely essential to seeing and entering the Kingdom of God.

II. WHEN CAN A PERSON BE BORN AGAIN?

The answer to this can be obtained by consulting your watch! The new birth takes place the moment a guilty sinner looks to Christ and trusts Him as his Lord and Savior. Why not, just where you are, and as you are, cease from your own efforts to save yourself, and trust in the Person and rest in the work of the Son of God, who did it all for you. (See II Corinthians 6:1, 2; Hebrews 4:7).

Come as a sinner, and trust now in Christ,
Who bore thy sins and shame;
Then, by the Spirit of God through the Word,
Thou shalt be born again!

Chapter 8

SALVATION

CLOSELY LINKED with the subject of the new birth is that of salvation. The former concerns itself principally with the necessity, source and *nature* of the spiritual life all men need from God; the latter emphasizes the delivering *effects* and *scope* of God's provision in Christ. We shall think of seven things in connection with salvation.

I. ITS DEFINITION

The word simply means deliverance. It is commonly used to describe the act by which a person is delivered from a danger which threatens him. We speak of a person being "saved" from drowning, or from a burning building, or from a sinking ship. In each case, three things are taken for granted. (1) The person to be saved was in danger of death. (2) Someone saw his peril and went to his rescue. (3) The rescuer was successful in his mission and delivered the person from his perilous plight, and thus "saved" him. The words: "save," "saved," "Savior," and "salvation" occur very many times in the Bible and have exactly the same meaning in a *spiritual* sense.

II. ITS NECESSITY

The necessity for God's salvation is due to two facts which each person must face.

1. *The fact of man's sin.* We have already discussed in our previous lesson, the spiritual condition of all men by nature, and we pointed out that each human being comes into the world possessed of a sinful nature that constitutes him a sinner by birth. This sinful nature, in time, is evidenced by sinful thoughts, words, deeds and attitude of enmity to God. The Bible makes this abundantly clear. Read Romans 5:12, 18, 19; 6:16; 8:5-8; Genesis 6:5; Ephesians 2:1-3; II Corinthians 4:3, 4; Isaiah 53:6; Jeremiah 17:9; Mark 7:20-23; Romans 1:21-32; 3:19-23. It will be evident to all from these Scriptures that man is: (1) A sinner, needing forgiveness. (2) Lost, needing to be found. (3) Doomed, needing deliverance. (4) Guilty, needing pardon. (5) Spiritually dead, needing life. (6)

Blind, needing illumination. (7) A slave, needing liberation. Man is thus utterly helpless to save himself.

2. *The fact of God's righteousness.* God is holy, and must punish sin. He will "by no means clear the guilty" (Exodus 34:6, 7). He has revealed His hatred of sin, and His sentence against all who die in their sins. This is eternal banishment from His presence. See John 8:21, 24; Mark 9:43-48; Luke 16:22-31; Jude 11-13; Revelation 20:11-15. The obvious conclusion is: Since man is a sinner, and God is righteous; the sinner needs to be delivered or saved from the penalty of his sins. His cry should be: "What must I do to be saved?" (Acts 16:30, 31).

III. ITS PROVISION

The Gospel is the good news that God in wondrous grace has abundantly provided this salvation through the Person and the work of His beloved Son. Two things are clearly taught.

1. *Christ came to be the Savior of sinners.* Matthew 1:21. The Son of God, equal and eternal with the Father and the Holy Spirit, became incarnate in order to provide salvation. John 3:16,

17; Mark 10:45; Matthew 9:12, 13; John 10:11, 15-18.

2. *Through Christ's death and resurrection, this salvation has been provided,* to God's complete satisfaction. As Christ willingly hung upon the cross, He assumed the full liability of our guilt and sin, bore our sins in His own body, and died as a substitutionary sacrifice on behalf of sinners. All God's judgment against sin fell on Him, and all God's righteous claims against the sinner were *fully satisfied* by Christ's death on our behalf. God indicated His complete acceptance of this sacrifice of Christ by raising Him from the dead and seating Him at His own right hand. Read I Corinthians 15:1-4; II Corinthians 5:21; I Peter 2:24; Isaiah 53:5; Romans 5:6-9; Acts 4:10-12; 5:31; 17:31.

IV. ITS CONDITION

Since Christ has accomplished, by the sacrifice of Himself, *all the work needed* for the sinner's salvation, what must the sinner do in order to experience this salvation?

1. *He must repent.* Repentance consists simply of a change of *mind* which results in a change of *attitude* toward sin, self, the Savior and salvation;

which, in turn, is evidenced by a change of *action.* Read Luke 13:3; Acts 17:31; 20:21. The sinner's indifference will give place to an earnest desire for salvation; his pride to humility; his self-satisfaction to a frank confession of his helpless, hopeless and hell-deserving condition.

2. *He must believe the gospel,* or the testimony of God concerning the Person and work of Christ. See I John 5:9-10. As a lost and guilty sinner he must believe that Christ died for him, individually; that Christ bore his sins, took *his* place and, by His death, accomplished all the work needed for *his* salvation (Romans 4:5).

3. *He must accept the Lord Jesus Christ, by a definite act of his will as his own personal Savior, henceforth to own Him as the supreme Lord of his life* (John 1:12; Romans 10:9, 10; John 3:16; 5:24; 6:47; Ephesians 1:13). This is the crucial act. Will you not, right from your heart, say: "Lord Jesus Christ; owning myself to be a guilty, lost sinner; but believing that Thou didst bear my sins and die in my place on Calvary; I now definitely rest in Thy finished work and receive Thee as my own Savior, henceforth to own Thee as the Lord and Master of my life." This is what it means

to "believe on the Lord Jesus Christ" (Acts 16: 31).

V. ITS ASSURANCE

How may one know, for certain, that he is saved? We answer without any hesitation: by the Word of God. God declares plainly and in black and white, that every soul trusting in His Son is forgiven, saved, the possessor of eternal life and secure forever. Read Acts 13:38; I John 2:12; Ephesians 2:8; I Corinthians 6:11; I John 5:13; Romans 5:1; 8:1; John 10:27-30.

VI. ITS SCOPE

Salvation has a three-fold aspect: past, present and future.

1. *Past.* Salvation from sin's *penalty*, or *consequences.* Since Christ has endured the full penalty which was due to our sins, the believer is delivered from its dread consequences. See John 5:24; Romans 8:1.

2. *Present.* Salvation from sin's *power,* or *control.* Because of the Holy Spirit's indwelling presence, plus the impartation of a Divine nature, the believer is now enabled to enjoy deliverance from the dominion of sin in his life (I Corinthians

6:19; II Peter 1:3, 4; Romans 6:1-14). This does not mean that the believer is incapable of sin; far from it, for he still possesses the evil nature called "the flesh." It does mean, however, that, in the measure that he avails himself of the means God has provided, sin shall not be the *dominating factor* in his life. This present deliverance will depend on: (1) The reading and study of and obedience to the Word of God (II Timothy 2:15). (2) The keeping constantly in touch with God by prayer (Hebrews 4:14-16). (3) The yielding of one's body to God for both a righteous and useful life (Romans 6:13; 12:1, 2). (4) The prompt confession to God and the forsaking of all known sin (I John 1:8, 9; Titus 2:11-15).

3. *Future.* Salvation from sin's *presence,* or *committal.* This will take place at the coming of Christ, when He will raise the dead and change the living, so that they will have bodies incapable of sin, decay and death. This is the final aspect of salvation that we look for (Hebrews 9:28; I Thessalonians 4:13-18).

VII. ITS RESULTS

These are multitudinous (Ephesians 1:3-14). We shall select a few.

1. *Peace with God.* Romans 5:1. No longer at enmity.

2. *Acceptance before God in Christ.* Ephesians 1:6.

3. *Joy in God as His children.* Romans 5:10, 11; 8:14-17; Galatians 3:26-4:7.

4. *Living for God.* II Corinthians 5:14, 15; Galatians 2:20; I Peter 4:2-5.

5. *Service to God* in the way of good works and testimony for Him. Ephesians 2:10; Matthew 5:16; Mark 16:15, 16.

6. *Worship, praise and prayer unto God.* John 4:23, 24; Hebrews 10:19-22; Hebrews 13:15; 4:14-16.

7. *An eternal home in heaven.* John 14:1-3; Revelation 22:1-5.

May each reader give himself no rest until he knows, on the authority of the Word of God, that he is eternally saved!

Chapter 9

GRACE

I. INTRODUCTION

ALL GOD'S DEALINGS with mankind at the present time are on the basis of grace. This means that He shows men favor which they do not deserve.

The word *grace* is found over 160 times in the Bible. Of these occurrences, 128 are in the New Testament. God is spoken of as "the God of all grace." I Peter 5:10. Christ is described as being "full of grace." John 1:14. The Holy Spirit is called "the Spirit of grace." Hebrews 10:29. Thus the three persons of the Godhead are closely linked with grace.

II. DEFINITION

The word used in the Old Testament carries the meaning—"to bend or stoop in kindness to an inferior." The New Testament word means—"favor, goodwill, lovingkindness."

The following definitions have proved helpful in explaining what grace is.

> Grace is love displayed to unworthy objects. God is love; but when He bestows that love on guilty, unclean, rebellious sinners, then it is grace.
>
> Love that looks up is adoration. Love on its own level is affection. Love that descends is grace.
>
> Grace is God showing nothing but love and mercy when we deserved nothing but wrath and judgment. It is God bending toward us in infinite love.
>
> Grace is seen in God giving heaven's Best to save earth's worst.

III. CONTRAST

Grace is not to be confused with works. If man could obtain salvation by doing good works, then salvation would simply be his wages. Romans 4:4-5. Romans 11:6. God does not owe anything to man. Salvation is a free gift.

Grace is not to be confused with law. Men are not saved by keeping the law. They are saved by grace. The following will help to make this clear.

(a) Law brings a work to do.

Grace tells of a work that is done.

(b) Law says, "This do and thou shalt live."

Grace says, "Live, and thou shalt do."

(c) Law says, "Thou shalt love the Lord thy God."

Grace says, "God so loved the world," John 3:16, and "We love Him because He first loved us." I John 4:19.

(d) Law condemns the best. Romans 3:19.

Grace saves the worst. Romans 3:24; 4:5.

(e) Law reveals sin. Romans 3:20.

Grace reveals salvation. Titus 2:11-13.

IV. THE NEED FOR GRACE

Man is a sinful rebel against God's holy law (Romans 3:23; Colossians 1:21). Therefore, he deserves nothing but God's judgment.

Man stands guilty before the bar of God, having broken God's holy law. (Romans 3:19; Galatians 3:10; James 2:10.) As such, he is subject to the curse of God.

Because he rejected and murdered God's Son, man has no claim on God at all. (John 12:31-33; 3:18.)

V. SALVATION BY GRACE

If man is to be saved, it must be by God's grace.

But God is holy and He cannot overlook sin. Sin must be punished.

The Gospel tells us how God can save sinners by grace, and still be holy in doing so. Christ suffered the wrath and judgment of God against sin. On the basis of the work of Christ, God can forgive the sins of those who trust the Lord Jesus.

Christ has finished the work. Grace only demands faith on the part of the sinner who seeks salvation. Ephesians 2:8, 9.

VI. BLESSINGS THROUGH GRACE

Grace brings many wonderful results to the sinner. Three of the greatest of these results are the following:

(a) Salvation. Titus 2:11-13. This means that a Christian has eternal life.

(b) Justification. Romans 3:24-26. This means that God reckons a sinner who has believed on Christ as being blameless.

(c) Standing before God. Romans 5:2. This means that a true believer can enter into God's presence by prayer. He is no longer separated from God by his sins.

Chapter 10

FAITH

ONE DOES NOT STUDY the Bible very long before becoming conscious of the importance of faith. A sinner cannot be saved apart from faith. Ephesians 2:8, 9. Therefore it is important that we should find out what this word means.

I. WHAT IS FAITH?

Faith is personal confidence. We use the word in everyday conversation, as follows, "I have complete faith in my doctor." We mean that we trust him with our case. So, in the Bible, faith is personal confidence in God. It means that we believe what He says, and trust Him to save us and to keep us.

II. WHERE DOES FAITH COME FROM?

As we look around us in the world, we realize

that some men do not have faith in God, and thus they are not saved. This leads us to inquire as to the source of faith. In a very real sense, this faith is a gift of God. John 3:27. God gives men the power to believe on Him.

But how does a man receive faith? The answer to this is found in Romans 10:17. "So then faith cometh by hearing, and hearing by the Word of God." Therefore, if a man does not have faith in God, he should read the Bible. As he reads, he should pray somewhat as follows: "God, if this Book is Thy Word, if Jesus Christ is Thy Son, and if He died for me, then show me these things as I read the Bible." God has promised that any man who wishes to do His will will come to a knowledge of the truth. John 7:17.

III. WHAT IS THE TRUE OBJECT OF FAITH?

Faith must have an object. This object may either be a person, such as a relative, or a friend, or it may be an inanimate thing, such as an airplane, or an elevator.

It is not enough to have faith. Faith must be placed in a trustworthy object. A man may have faith in his automobile to take him to a certain place, but if the automobile is badly in need of repairs, he will soon find that his faith has been misplaced.

The Bible sets forth the Lord Jesus Christ as the true object of faith. Acts 20:21. The important thing is not how much faith a man has, or what kind of faith he has, but whether his faith is in Christ. If it is, then the man is saved.

A man may believe all that the Bible says about Christ and yet not have faith in Him. You may believe that a certain train will leave the railroad station at 11 A.M. and that it will arrive at a distant city at 5 P.M. You may believe all the facts *about* the train; yet you do not really believe *in* the train, until you get on board, and trust the train to take you to your destination.

So you may believe that Christ was born in Bethlehem, that He died on Calvary, that He rose again and ascended into heaven. But you have not really put your faith in Him until you trust Him to save you from your sins and take you to heaven.

IV. EXAMPLES OF FAITH

The Scriptures are filled with examples of faith. The eleventh chapter of Hebrews has been called the "Honor Roll of Faith" because it lists some outstanding men and women who had faith.

Two other instances might be cited. The first is the faith of the centurion in Matthew 8:5-10. The centurion believed that Christ could heal his servant by merely saying the word.

The other is the faith of the woman of Canaan, Matthew 15:22-28. She pleaded that the bread reserved for the chosen Jews should be given to her, a Gentile. Her faith was humble and persistent.

V. THE REWARD OF FAITH

True faith never goes unrewarded. No one has ever trusted God in vain. Every seeking sinner who has repented of his sins and who has put his faith in the Lord Jesus Christ has been saved.

The Savior said, "Him that cometh to me, I will in no wise cast out." John 6:37.

Chapter 11

HEAVEN AND HELL

MEN HAVE ALWAYS had a sincere interest in the future. This interest has aroused questions such as the following: Does death end all? Where are the dead? What can we know about heaven and hell? First, we shall consider the question:

I. WHAT HAPPENS TO A MAN AT THE TIME OF DEATH?

At the outset, we need to remember that man is a tripartite being, that is, he is composed of three parts—body, soul, and spirit. I Thessalonians 5:23. The first part is material being, the other two are non-material. With a spirit, man is capable of God-consciousness; with a soul, he is capable of self-consciousness; with a body, he is capable of world-consciousness. Only God's Word can divide between the soul and the spirit. Hebrews 4:12.

Now, at the time of death, the soul and spirit leave the body. The body is put into the grave. In the case of believers, the body is described as sleeping (Acts 7:59, 60; 8:2), while the unsaved person's body is spoken of as dead. The soul and spirit never sleep. If the person who died was saved, the soul and the spirit go to a place of joy and happiness—heaven (II Cor. 5:8; Phil. 1:21, 23). If the person was unsaved, the spirit and soul go to a place of sorrow and punishment—hades. In Luke 16:19-31, our Lord clearly teaches that those who have died are conscious. Be sure to read this important passage.

II. WHAT DO WE KNOW ABOUT HELL?

As we have already noted, the spirit and soul of an unbeliever wing their flight to hades at the time of death. Hades is a place of conscious punishment (Luke 16:23-25; the Revised Version correctly uses "hades" for "hell" in v. 23). The soul in hades is spoken of as a person, having eyes, tongue, ears, fingers and memory. There is full knowledge of the conditions there.

The Bible speaks about another place of torment

in addition to hades. That other place is hell—the Lake of Fire. At the Judgment of the Great White Throne, which will be discussed in the next chapter, the souls in hades will be united with the bodies which are to be raised from the graves. Christ will then pronounce the final sentence of judgment upon the wicked dead, and they will be cast into the Lake of Fire, the eternal abode of the lost (Rev. 20:11-15). Hades may thus be likened to the local jail where the prisoner temporarily awaits his sentence. The Lake of Fire may be likened to a prison to which are committed those under sentence for the duration of their earthly existence. In describing hell, our Lord speaks about the undying worm and the unquenchable fire (Mark 9:43-48). It is a place of conscious punishment.

Is punishment for sin eternal? In the book of Revelation, the phrase "forever and ever" is used to describe the misery of the lost. Revelation 14:11.

Can a God of love allow men to go to hell? (1) God does not want men to perish. He provided for man's salvation through the work of His Son on Calvary's Cross. Romans 5:6, 8. If men reject the

Savior, they go to hell by their own choice. (2) God is a God of love, I John 4:8, but He is also holy, I Peter 1:16. He must punish sin. (3) Men do not hesitate to put sick people in hospitals, criminals in jail, or corpses in the cemetery. This does not indicate a lack of love on their part.

What about the heathen who has never heard the Gospel? Like the rest of mankind, heathens are lost sinners, and only Christ can save them. They can tell that there is a God through the works of creation, Romans 1:20 and Psalm 19:1; and through their own consciences, Romans 2:15. If they live up to the light which they have, God will give them more light—see Cornelius, Acts 10 and 11.

III. WHAT DO WE KNOW ABOUT HEAVEN?

The Scriptures clearly teach that there is a place of bliss for all who know and love our Lord Jesus Christ. Heaven is a place. The word is used in the Bible in three different ways. First of all, the region of the clouds is called heaven. Genesis 1:8. Then the area where the stars are located is known as heaven. Genesis 1:17. Finally, the word is used to describe God's dwelling place. Paul calls this the "third heaven" and "Paradise." II Corinthians 12:2-4. Heaven is always mentioned as being "up." Satan said, in Isaiah 14:13-14, "I will ascend into heaven."

We know that our Lord is in heaven today. After He was raised from the dead, He ascended in a body of flesh and bones. He carried glorified humanity into heaven. Luke 24:38, 39, 51; I Peter 3:22; Hebrews 1:3.

There is a great host of believers in heaven, for when the true Christian dies, he is "absent from the body—present with the Lord." II Corinthians 5:8. These believers are enjoying the presence of Christ "which is very far better." Philippians 1:23.

What is heaven like? The writers of the Scriptures could not find language that would describe it. In Revelation 21:10-27, John describes the foundations, wall, gates, and street of the heavenly city. Our hearts are attracted by its beauty. We know that there will be no sickness, sorrow, tears, pain or death in that fair place. Revelation 21:4. But best of all, the Lord Jesus Christ will be there, and He will be the supreme delight of every believer's heart.

Chapter 12

FUTURE EVENTS

EVERY BIBLE student is thrilled to be able to read about events that are still future. Only in the Bible is the future unfolded. In this lesson, we shall consider some of these events in the order in which they will happen.

I. CHRIST'S COMING FOR HIS SAINTS

I Thessalonians 4:13-18

The next event to occur is the coming of Christ to take His people home to heaven. This is known as the Rapture. Christ will descend from heaven. The bodies of believers who have died will be raised. Living believers will be caught up together with them to meet the Lord in the air.

Note the following facts about the coming of Christ.

1. It may happen at any moment. Revelation 22:7.

2. Only those who are truly saved will participate. I Corinthians 15:23.

3. It takes place instantly,—"in the twinkling of an eye." I Corinthians 15:52.

4. Not all believers will die but all will be changed. I Corinthians 15:51. They shall be like Christ. I John 3:2; Romans 8:16-25.

II. THE TRIBULATION

Matthew 24:5-31

After the Rapture, the earth will experience a period of great suffering and sorrow known as the Tribulation. During this period, the Jewish people will return to the land of Palestine in unbelief. A great evil ruler will arise known as Antichrist (meaning against-Christ). He will demand worship from the people. It will be a time of such great suffering that unless the days were shortened, no life would survive. However, God will preserve those Jewish people who have been faithful to Him.

III. CHRIST'S COMING TO REIGN

Malachi 4:1-3

Toward the end of the Tribulation period, the

Lord Jesus Christ will come back to the earth in great power and glory. He will destroy His enemies, including Antichrist, and judge those nations which persecuted faithful Jews. Satan will be bound in the bottomless pit for 1000 years.

IV. THE MILLENNIUM

Isaiah 32:1; 35:1-7; 65:17-25

When His work of judgment has been completed, Christ will set up His kingdom on the earth. Jerusalem will be His capital. He will reign upon the earth for a thousand years. This period is known as the millennium. It will be an era of peace and happiness. We read that nature will be entirely different, for the lion will lie down with the lamb. The desert will blossom like the rose. Men will live to very old ages. It will be a time of great prosperity. There will be no wars. Although sin will not be entirely absent, it will be punished immediately whenever it occurs.

V. THE JUDGMENT OF THE GREAT WHITE THRONE

Revelation 20:11-15

At the end of Christ's 1000-year reign, the Judgment of the Great White Throne will take place. This is the judgment of the wicked dead. No saved persons will be involved. The graves will give up the bodies of unbelievers, and hades or hell will give up their souls. They will then stand before Christ to be judged. Because their names are not found in the Lamb's book of life, they will be found guilty and sentenced to the Lake of Fire to suffer conscious and eternal punishment.

VI. ETERNITY

Revelation 21:1-8

The final picture of the future is the eternal state. The earth as we know it will have been destroyed by fire. Time, as we know it, will have ceased. All true believers will be enjoying endless happiness in heaven. All who have rejected the Savior will be suffering in the blackness of darkness forever. The question that faces each one of us as we draw to the end of these Bible studies is this, "Where will I spend eternity?"

THE CHRISTIAN LIFE

Chapter 13

RESULTS OF REGENERATION

WHAT ACTUALLY HAPPENS when a person is born again? Here is what takes place when a soul is born again. First, the person realizes that he is a lost sinner and that he deserves to spend eternity in hell. (Only the Holy Spirit can make anyone realize this.) He then repents of his sins, that is, he acknowledges to God that he is a sinner and that he needs a Savior. He accepts Jesus Christ as his Lord and Savior, and at that moment he is born again. His sins are forgiven. He receives eternal life from God.

But that is only a small part of the story. It is just the beginning. We learn from the Bible that many other wonderful things occur when God saves a man. Here are ten other amazing occurrences:

1. For one thing, *the believer is accepted in the*

Beloved One (Ephesians 1:6). This means that he stands before God in all the acceptability of His Beloved Son. God sees him in Christ (II Corinthians 5:17). It also means that the Christian is welcome in God's presence as long as Christ is welcome, and that is clearly forever (Ephesians 2:6, 7).

2. Also, *he becomes a child of God* (John 1:12). You can imagine how honored you would feel if you were the child of some world-famous ruler. How much greater honor it is to be the child of the mighty Maker of the universe, before whom angels bow! (Galatians 3:26).

3. *He is justified by God* (Romans 5:1; 8:30, 33). God, the Judge, declares the believing sinner to be "NOT GUILTY" and looks upon him as if he had never sinned. He can do this because Christ has died as a substitute and has borne all the punishment which the Christian should have borne. Thus the Christian stands without guilt in God's sight, and he will never be punished for his sins (Romans 8:1).

4. *He becomes indwelt by the Holy Spirit* (I Corinthians 6:19). The Bible plainly teaches that God, the Holy Spirit, actually dwells within each believer (I John 4:13). The body of the Christian

is the temple of the Holy Spirit. Because of this sacred privilege, the child of God should be careful what he says, what he does and where he goes.

5. *He becomes a member of the true church* (I Corinthians 12:13). The church is described as "the body of Christ" (Colossians 1:18, 24). It is composed of all true believers in the Lord Jesus (Acts 2:47). There is no greater honor on earth than to be a member of the true church.

6. *He becomes an heir of God* (Romans 8:17). God is the Creator of the universe and He owns all things. God's children are promised that they will one day reign with Christ over all the earth, and they will then possess all things.

7. *He becomes a saint* (Romans 1:7). Those who are saved are spoken of in the Bible as "saints." A saint is one who has been set apart for God by the Holy Spirit (Psalm 4:3). In God's sight every saint is holy, because God sees him in Christ, and Christ is absolutely holy (I Corinthians 1:2).

8. *He is complete in Christ* (Colossians 2:10). The Christian has a perfect standing before God. He is as near and as dear to God as Christ is. When a person has Christ, he has all that he needs for a happy life and a happy eternity.

9. *He receives the divine nature* (II Peter 1:4). He will soon notice that he has new desires, new ambitions, a new hatred of sin, and a new love for his fellow Christians. When the divine nature is encouraged by the believer himself, he will become more and more like the Lord Jesus (Colossians 3:10; II Corinthians 3:18). This is God's purpose for every one of His children.

10. *He immediately begins to enjoy the constant protection of God* (Romans 8:28). Nothing can happen to a Christian without God's permission. In other words, there are no accidents in a believer's life. Everything that does happen to a child of God is for his own good. Even trials, tests and disciplines work for his spiritual benefit (Romans 5:3-5). Thus a Christian truly leads a "charmed" life.

In view of these marvelous provisions which God has made, every Christian should show his appreciation in at least two ways.

1. He should never cease to worship God for salvation through the Lord Jesus Christ.
2. He should give his life in willing service to the One who gave His life on Calvary's Cross (Romans 12:1).

Chapter 14

SURE SALVATION

HOW CAN A PERSON know for certain that he is saved? Read the following facts over and over until you fully understand them.

1. The Bible is God's Word. It is absolutely true. You can trust it.

2. The Bible says that if you repent of your sins and believe on the Lord Jesus Christ, you are saved.

3. Now the question is "Have you ever come to Christ as a lost sinner, and asked Him to save you? Have you ever accepted Him as the Substitute who bore the penalty of your sins?"

4. If you have, then God tells you in the Bible that you are saved.

In other words,—and this is very important to understand—*assurance of salvation comes through the Scriptures*. This truth is clearly taught in I John 5:13. Every Christian should memorize this verse.

> These things have I written unto you that believe on the name of the Son of God; that ye may *know* that ye have eternal life, and that ye may believe on the name of the Son of God.

Notice the *italicized* word. John wrote to those who had believed on Christ so that they might *know* that they had eternal life. If you have believed on Christ, you are saved. The Bible says so.

The trouble with so many is that they depend on feelings rather than on the Bible. They say, "I do not feel saved." They expect some mysterious emotional experience, and when they do not receive it, they doubt that they were ever saved. The person who bases his assurance of salvation on his feelings is certain to have difficulty because feelings change from moment to moment. God's Word, however, never changes. Trust the Bible and not your feelings.

But perhaps someone will ask, "Shouldn't a person feel happy when he is saved?" The answer is definitely "Yes." However, one must *know* he is saved before he can *feel* happy. Assurance comes first, then feelings follow. We know we are saved because the Bible says so. We feel happy because we know we are saved.

In addition to the Scriptures themselves, there are other means of assurance for the believer. Here are three marks of a saved person:

1. The person who is saved loves his fellow Christians (I John 3:14).

2. The person who is saved has the witness of the Holy Spirit within him (I John 5:10; Romans 8:16). The witness of the Spirit is the inner joy and peace which is given to those who believe the Word of God when it says that all who believe on Christ are saved. The Spirit witnesses to Christians through the Bible.

3. The person who is saved hates sin and loves what is right. Although a Christian can and does sin, sin no longer controls his life (Romans 6:14). He no longer lives in the continual practice of sin.

As a believer grows in the Christian life, his assurance will become stronger and stronger. There are at least three definite steps which he may take to help in this direction.

1. Read the Bible regularly and believe it with all your heart.

2. Pray to the Lord to strengthen your faith as you read His Holy Word.

3. Tell others about the One who has saved you from sin.

Finally, there is a helpful bit of advice for those who are not sure if they were ever saved, but who really want to be. Perhaps you think you might have trusted the Savior sometime in the past, but you are not absolutely certain. You long to know without any doubt that you are a child of God.

Here is what you should do. Tell the Lord that you are not sure if you were ever saved before, but you want to be saved right now. Tell Him that you know you are a lost sinner and that if you die in your present condition, you will go to hell. Then receive the Lord Jesus Christ as your Savior, believing that He died on Calvary's Cross to pay the penalty of your sins, and that He is able and willing to save you.

Now turn to Acts 16:31. What does it say will happen if you believe on the Lord Jesus Christ? It says, "Thou shalt be saved." It is the Word of God. Believe it. When Satan comes to you and tries to make you doubt your salvation, turn to Acts 16:31, or John 1:12, or John 3:36, or John 5:24, or Romans 10:9. Show him that God says you are saved because you have believed on Christ. He will not trouble you with doubts if you show him the Scriptures.

Chapter 15

PERMANENT PRESERVATION

CAN A SAVED PERSON ever perish? If a person has been truly born again, he can never perish. The believer is safe and secure forever. Seven passages of Scripture are listed below as evidence of this glorious truth, though many more could be given. (The student should study each quotation carefully.)

1. John 10:27-29. Notice these words of Christ, "I give unto them eternal life, and *they shall never perish.*" Plant your feet on that. This is the promise of Christ without any conditions attached. No sheep of His will ever perish! Notice, too, that both Christ and the Father hold you securely.

2. John 5:24. Here again the Lord Jesus Christ is speaking. He promises that the person who hears His Word and believes on the One who sent Him

has everlasting life, and will never come into condemnation, or judgment. If one believer were ever lost, then the Son of God would have failed to keep His promise.

3. John 3:36. "He that believeth on the Son hath everlasting life." Notice that it does not say, "he *will have* everlasting life." He has it at the present time. Now, how long is "everlasting"? Clearly it is forever.

4. Romans 8:38, 39. The Apostle Paul announces that neither death, life, angels, principalities, powers, things present, things to come, height nor depth can separate the Christian from the love of God. And lest any child of God might worry that *he might separate himself* from the love of God, Paul adds, "nor any other creature." The believer is as safe as God can make him.

5. II Timothy 1:12. Paul here expresses his confidence that Christ is able to keep what Paul had committed to Him, that is, his soul. In John 6:39, we learn that God has entrusted Christ with the preservation of *all* believers. Is it possible that Christ could be unfaithful to His trust?

6. Jude 24. The Lord Jesus is the One who is able to keep Christians from falling, and to take

them safely home to heaven. Christians are no more able to keep themselves saved than they were to save themselves in the first place, but Christ is able (I Peter 1:5).

7. Romans 8:30. "Whom He justified, them He also glorified." Every saved person is glorified. Although Christians do not yet have their glorified bodies, yet it is so certain that God speaks of it as an accomplished fact. If you are justified, then, as far as God is concerned, you are glorified too. In other words, the Christian is just as sure of heaven as if he were already there.

In connection with the subject of the Christian's security, the following facts should be remembered.

1. A Christian does not lose his salvation when he sins. Christ has already paid the penalty for all his sins—past, present and future. God will not demand payment twice. Since Christ has died for my sins, I will never have to die for them. God the righteous Judge, forgives the sinner who believes on Christ.

2. But when a Christian does sin, he displeases his heavenly Father, and the happy family spirit that should exist between the child and his Father remains broken until that sin is confessed (I John

1:9). Notice clearly that there is a big difference between God, the *Judge*, dealing with a sinner, and God the *Father* dealing with an erring child. In the former case, the penalty for sin is death and hell. In the latter case, the result of sin is broken fellowship (I John 2:1, 2).

3. Even the Christian cannot sin cheaply. If a child of God wanders away from his Father, he can expect to be corrected (Hebrews 12:6, 7). The Father might use sorrow or suffering to bring him back. In some cases, God even takes the believer home to heaven: his body dies, but his soul is saved (I Corinthians 5:5).

4. While a Christian can and does, unfortunately, commit acts of sin, no true child of God lives a life of continual sin. "A Christian is not sinless, but he does sin less." If a person can keep on sinning without being brought back to fellowship with God through chastenings, it is a sure sign that he was never born again. Our security must not be an excuse to sin, but rather an incentive not to sin.

5. There are several verses in the Bible which might seem to indicate that Christians can be lost again. However, if you examine them carefully,

you will find that they refer to those who merely pretend to be Christians, or to those who have known the way of salvation and have rejected it. Nowhere do the Scriptures say that a truly born-again person can perish. It is only such persons who are secure.

Chapter 16

TRIUMPH OVER TEMPTATION

How can a Christian resist sinful temptations? Whenever a person is saved, a great struggle begins. He still has the old nature, the sinful nature of Adam, which will try to drag him into sin all the time. But he also has the new nature, the life of God, which hates sin and wants to do what is right. The two natures fight against each other continually (Galatians 5:16, 17; Romans 8:5-8).

The old nature is incurably bad. It cannot be improved, and it will not be removed until the Christian goes home to heaven. God condemned it when Christ died on the Cross, and He wants Christians to treat it as if it were dead. Don't encourage it! Don't feed it! Don't give it a chance! (Romans 13:14).

The new nature inspires the Christian to do good. It should be encouraged and fed.

This, then, is how the Christian resists temptation—by saying "No" to the flesh, or old nature, and by nourishing the new life that is within. The following are practical suggestions as to how this may be done:

1. Read the Bible! Study it! Memorize it! Meditate on it! Obey it! Notice Psalm 119:9 and 11. There we learn that the Word of God helps to keep us from sinning. Be sure, therefore, that you set aside a definite time each day for the reading of God's Word (Colossians 3:16).

2. Pray without ceasing! Whenever you are faced with temptation, ask God for help (Hebrews 4:16). He will give you the strength to overcome (I Corinthians 10:13). If you try to resist by your own strength, you will surely fail.

3. Seek the companionship of fellow-believers and not of the ungodly! (Proverbs 1:10-16; Hebrews 10:24, 25). It is often necessary to work and live with unbelievers, and in such cases we should witness to them both with our lips and by our lives. But we should not join with them in their worldly pleasures and amusements (Ephesians 5:11).

4. Confess your sins immediately! As soon as you are conscious that you have grieved your Father by a sinful thought, word or deed, ask His forgiveness immediately. Do not wait until evening or until the end of the week (Proverbs 28: 13).

5. Keep busy for the Lord! Someone has said that idle hands are the devil's workshop. Give your body to the Lord to use it as He desires! (Romans 6:19). There is plenty of work to be done, and you will be serving the Best of Masters.

6. Engage in some physical exercise! Bodily exercise is profitable (I Timothy 4:8). Because the believer's body is the temple of the Holy Spirit, he should use reasonable means in maintaining his body in good health and strength. However, he should not allow sports to assume such an important place that spiritual things are crowded out (I Corinthians 6:19, 20).

7. Starve the old nature! Be careful what you read, what you watch, where you go, and what you listen to (Colossians 3:5-9).

8. Feed the new nature! Be occupied with Christ! When you are thinking about Him, you cannot be thinking about sin (Colossians 3:10-14). This is really the secret of holy living—occupation

with Christ. It is a fixed rule in life that we become like the object of our worship. II Corinthians 3:18 teaches us that we become like the Lord Jesus as we behold Him in the mirror (glass) of His Word. We are changed into His image and likeness by the Holy Spirit who dwells within us.

> Occupation with others brings distraction.
> Occupation with self brings distress.
> Occupation with Christ brings delight.

One final word! You will notice from the foregoing that deliverance from temptation is not a once-for-all experience, but a continual process of depending on God. No matter how old we get, or how much we may learn about the Bible, we are still in danger of yielding to temptation if we take our eyes off the Lord. A very godly man used to pray that God would keep him from dying as a wicked old man. We all need to pray the same petition (Colossians 3:1-4).

Chapter 17

CHRISTIAN CONDUCT

HOW CAN A CHRISTIAN know what he may or may not do? Is it all right for a believer to go to dances or to the theatre, to play cards, to smoke, to drink or to participate in other worldly pleasures and amusements?

Many young converts are troubled by questions similar to the above. They find that certain practices are clearly condemned in the Bible, but that there are many others which are not mentioned. It is the purpose of this lesson to provide the student with a series of standards which may help him to decide whether or not he should engage in a questionable activity.

1. First of all, is it distinctly forbidden by the Lord for believers today? If it is, avoid it as you would a deadly plague. If you do not know, don't

do it until you have had a chance to find out (I Thessalonians 5:22).

2. Then, is there any glory for God in it? In I Corinthians 10:31, we read this plain statement: "Whatsoever ye do, do all to the glory of God." Before you engage in the activity in question, can you honestly ask for God's blessing upon it, believing that He will be honored through your participation?

3. Is it "of the world"? If it is, then it is not "of Christ." He said concerning His disciples, "They are not of the world, even as I am not of the world" (John 17:16). He was not "of the world" *at all*. He was *in it*, but not *of it* (I John 2:15-17).

4. Would the Lord have done it? He has left us an example that we should follow His steps (I Peter 2:21).

5. Would you like to be found doing it when the Lord returns? Someone has wisely remarked, "Don't do anything, say anything, or go anywhere that would cause you shame if the Lord should come!" (I John 2:28).

6. Can you feel free to do it when you remember that God the Holy Spirit dwells within you? "Know ye not that your body is the temple of the

Holy Ghost which is in you, which ye have of God, and ye are not your own?" (I Corinthians 6:19). See also Ephesians 4:30.

7. Is it fitting conduct for a child of God? When a king's son acts in an unworthy manner, he brings disgrace on his father's name. So does the Christian who behaves in an unbecoming way (Romans 2:24; Colossians 1:10).

8. What effect will your conduct have on others? Will it be a good testimony to the unsaved, or will they decide that there is really no difference between a Christian and an unbeliever (II Corinthians 5:17)? Also, will it cause someone who is young in the faith to stumble? The Apostle Paul warned that no man should put "a stumblingblock or an occasion to fall in his brother's way" (Romans 14:13).

9. Finally, is there the least bit of doubt in your mind about it? If so, then don't do it, for "he that doubteth is damned [condemned] . . . for whatsoever is not of faith is sin" (Romans 14:23).

In connection with this subject of what a Christian may or may not do, it is well to remember that "we are not under the law, but under grace" (Romans 6:14, 15). This does not mean that we may do as we like, but rather it means we want to do what God likes because He has done so much for us. We do not avoid worldly pleasures and amusements because we have to, but because we want to. The reason we want to is because Christ died for us, and now our ambitions are to live in a manner that will please Him (II Corinthians 5:14, 15). God does not say, "If you keep away from sinful pleasures, you will be a Christian." But He does say, in effect, to the believer, "You are a Christian! Now live in a way that is consistent with your high calling" (Ephesians 4:1).

It is possible that a Christian may forget his dignified position, and go in for the things of the world. In such a case, God will bring him back by loving correction, just as a shepherd brings back a wandering sheep by placing his crook around its neck. Thus, if God's *grace* is forgotten by the believer, he will be restored by God's *government*.

Chapter 18

BURIED IN BAPTISM

WHAT IS BAPTISM, and who should be baptized? Before the Lord Jesus ascended to heaven, He gave the Great Commission to His disciples: "Go ye therefore, and teach all nations, *baptizing them in the name of the Father, and of the Son, and of the Holy Ghost*: teaching them to observe all things whatsoever I have commanded you: and lo, I am with you alway, even unto the end of the world. Amen" (Matthew 28:19, 20).

It was thus the Lord's desire that, as His servants went throughout the world with the Gospel, they should baptize those who received the message. Baptism is an ordinance instituted by the Lord Himself. This raises two questions. First, how is the ordinance of baptism carried out? Second, what is the meaning of baptism?

In order to find a true answer to the first, we

shall turn to Acts 8:26-39. There we find a servant of the Queen of Ethiopia riding along in his chariot, and reading the book of Isaiah, chapter 53, in the Old Testament. This man was a sincere seeker for the truth, and so God instructed His servant, Philip, to speak with him. Philip told him how the Lord Jesus had died on Calvary so that sinners might be saved. The traveler believed on the Lord Jesus Christ, and then asked Philip if he could be baptized. Inasmuch as the man had truly believed on Christ, Philip agreed to baptize him. The chariot was therefore halted near a body of water. Now notice verses 38 and 39 carefully:

> . . . and they went down both into the water, both Philip and the eunuch; and he baptized him. And when they were come up out of the water, the Spirit of the Lord caught away Philip, that the eunuch saw him no more: and he went on his way rejoicing.

Now what is the true significance of this ceremony which was carried out so simply along that eastern highway many years ago, and which continues to be performed to this very day?

1. First of all, it is an act of obedience to the expressed will of the Lord Jesus (Matthew 28:19). Its purpose is not to put away the filth of the flesh, but rather to give the Christian a good conscience

toward God, knowing that he has obeyed the Lord's will (I Peter 3:21). Only those who have heard and believed should be baptized (Acts 18:8).

2. Secondly, Romans 6:3-5 teaches that it is a symbol or picture of a spiritual truth.

(a) The water is a picture of judgment and death.

(b) When Christ died, He went under the waters of judgment and death to put away our sins (Psalm 42:7).

(c) Since Christ died as a substitute for the believer, it is equally true that the believer died with the Lord Jesus. In other words, when Christ died, I died. When He was buried, I was buried. When He arose, I arose.

(d) The Christian has died to sin, to the world and to self. He has died to all that he was by nature, and from now on God no longer sees him in his sins, but sees him in Christ, risen from the dead, and possessing the resurrection life of Christ (Galatians 2:20).

(e) Thus, when a Christian is baptized, he is making a public confession that he has taken his place with Christ in death and burial, and that henceforth he shall seek to show to all that he possesses the life of Christ (Colossians 2:12; 3:1, 2).

3. The truly baptized person is the one who has not only been baptized in literal water, but whose life shows that the flesh, or old nature, has been put in the place of death. Baptism must be a matter of the heart, as well as an outward profession.

In the early days of the Church, when a believer was baptized, he was often persecuted and murdered in a short time. Yet whenever others were saved, they too stepped forward to fill up the ranks of the martyrs by being baptized (I Corinthians 15:29).

Even today in heathen lands, baptism is the signal for the beginning of terrible persecution. In many countries a believer will be tolerated as long as he confesses Christ only with his lips. But whenever he publicly confesses Christ in baptism, the enemies of the Cross take up their battle against him.

Yet whatever the cost may be, each one who is baptized enjoys the same experience that the Ethiopian eunuch did. It is written of him: "He went on his way *rejoicing*" (Acts 8:39).

Chapter 19

CHOOSING A CHURCH

HOW CAN A CHRISTIAN know which church to join? By way of introduction to this subject, it should be stated that a person is joined to the true church at the very moment of his conversion. This church is made up of every true believer on the Lord Jesus Christ, regardless of race, color or culture. Members of the church are found throughout the world, though the entire church has never yet been assembled in one place.

However, it is possible for Christians in any locality to gather together as members of the church, and perform the functions which are set forth in Scripture. In the early days, the saints met in their own homes (Romans 16:5; Philemon 2); and we read that "they continued steadfastly in the apostles' doctrine and fellowship, and in breaking of bread, and in prayers" (Acts 2:42).

Now it is very obviously the Lord's will that Christians should meet together regularly as members of the church. Hebrews 10:25 contains a warning against forsaking "the assembling of ourselves together, as the manner of some is." Moreover, great portions of the New Testament are devoted to teaching believers their privileges and responsibilities as members of the body of Christ (I Corinthians 12).

Yet it is somewhat of a problem for a new convert today to know where he should unite in fellowship. There are so many different groups of Christians, and such a wide difference in some of their teachings.

The following list is therefore designed to help the young believer in finding the right path. At the same time, it should be emphasized that the entire question should be made the matter of earnest prayer that God's will might be clearly known. Our understanding of what the church is must come from God's Word alone. Traditions and customs of men must be tested by its teachings on this subject (Isaiah 8:20).

1. Be sure that the group with whom you identify yourself acknowledges the Holy Bible as the inspired and infallible Word of God, and bows to

the Scriptures as the final authority in all matters of faith and practice. It is not enough to say that the Bible *contains* the Word of God. It *is* the Word of God. Therefore it is absolutely true, and we must believe it and obey it (II Timothy 3:16, 17).

2. Be sure that those with whom you meet are unmistakably clear as to the Person of Christ. Many are willing to admit that Christ was a great leader, the greatest man who ever lived, or they even use the word "divine" in describing Him. But the great truth concerning our blessed Savior is that He is God, and nothing less than this will do (Colossians 2:9).

3. A third important thing to watch for is sound teaching concerning the work of Christ. Scripture teaches that the Lord Jesus lived a sinless life, that He voluntarily died for our sins on the Cross of Calvary, that He was buried, that He rose again and ascended into heaven, where He is now seated at the right hand of God (I Corinthians 15:1-4). Salvation is obtained solely by faith in Him and quite apart from any works or human merit (Galatians 1:6-9). Be sure to find out what is taught concerning His precious blood. Apart from that blood there can be no remission of sins.

In addition to meeting the above three primary tests, one should be sure that the local church does not contradict, by word or by practice, the following important truths concerning the body of Christ.

1. *Christ is the Head of the church* (Colossians 1:18, 19; Ephesians 1:22, 23). No man may claim this position. Where Christ is acknowleged as Head, the church will look to Him and to Him alone for dictation and guidance.

2. *All believers are members of the body of Christ* (I Corinthians 12:12, 13). All true children of God should therefore be welcomed into the fellowship of the church. (There are, however, two exceptions to this rule. Those who are unsound in doctrine, II John 10, or who are living in sin, I Corinthians 5:13, should be excluded until they have been restored to the Lord.) No unbeliever should knowingly be received into church fellowship.

3. *All believers are priests* (I Peter 2:5, 9). In the New Testament, there is no distinction as to priests and people. All Christians may now enter by faith into the presence of God, bringing sacrifices of praise and worship and service. In the early church all the members were students of the Word, all were soul-winners, all were busy for

God. That should characterize the church today.

4. *The authority of the Holy Spirit should be recognized.* Whether in worship or in service, ministry or discipline, there should be liberty for the Holy Spirit to direct. His guidance and authority ought not to be limited by man-made ceremonies or human organization (II Corinthians 3:17; Ephesians 4:3).

To summarize, then, a young believer should fellowship with those who acknowledge the Bible as their only guide, who are sound as to the Person and work of Christ, and who seek to carry out the teachings of the New Testament with regard to the church and its functions.

Chapter 20

WANTING GOD'S WILL

How can a Christian know God's will in his life? Every Christian should be keenly interested in knowing God's will for his life. Unless the Lord's plan is known and obeyed, then our lives are wasted, and we will miss the Master's "Well done."

The Scriptures are emphatic in teaching that God does reveal His will to those who desire to know it (John 7:17). It is a privilege that should be the normal experience of every believer (Romans 12:2).

Whether one is seeking guidance as to a momentary problem or as to a life career, there are five steps to be followed. These may be summarized as follows: YIELD; CONFESS; PRAY; STUDY; WAIT.

1. YIELD. To yield is to present oneself to

the Lord. It means to lay aside personal hopes, ambitions and desires. It means to want His way supremely. Paul yielded when he asked, "What wilt thou have me to do?" Isaiah yielded when he said, "Here am I; send me." Amaziah yielded for we read that "he willingly offered himself unto the Lord" (II Chronicles 17:16).

2. CONFESS. If we want to be in the center of His will, we must confess and forsake any secret sins which we cherish. Remember the words of the Psalmist, "If I regard iniquity in my heart, the Lord will not hear me" (Psalm 66:18). We should also confess our own helplessness and inability, and depend on His power (Psalm 139:23, 24).

3. PRAY. This simply means that we must come before the Lord regularly, asking for His direction. We should claim His promise for guidance, asking Him to do as He has said. Our prayers should have His glory as their chief aim (Colossians 1:9; 4:12).

4. STUDY. Spend much time in the Word of God. Read it while you are on your knees, asking God to speak to you through it. Read it slowly. Read it thoughtfully. Read it expectantly. (Psalm 143:8, 10).

5. WAIT. If God does not answer immedi-

ately, wait (Psalm 62:6). If you have prayed for direction and no answer comes, then God's guidance is for you to stay where you are. If you are really trusting in the Lord, you will not be in a hurry. "He that believeth shall not make haste" (Isaiah 28:16). God reveals His will to us in several different ways. He may use one, or a combination, of the following methods:

1. *Guidance through the Bible.* The Scriptures give direction in two ways. First of all, they definitely prohibit certain courses of action. For instance, if a Christian were praying for guidance as to whether he should marry an unsaved girl, he could get God's answer in II Corinthians 6:14. On the other hand, God often uses other verses of Scripture to guide us to take a certain definite course of action. A verse that you had never noticed before may take on new meaning because it tells you what to do at the very time when you were praying for direction (Psalm 119:105).

2. *Guidance through Christians.* It is sometimes helpful to seek the advice of mature, spiritual Christians. Their experience and counsel can often save a younger person from serious pitfalls (Hebrews 13:7, 17).

3. *Guidance through circumstances.* Since God

controls the entire universe, He can and often does plan the circumstances of our lives to reveal His will. A letter, for instance, may arrive at just the right time with just the information needed to point the way.

4. *Guidance through the Holy Spirit.* The Spirit of God can influence our convictions, our desires or our inclinations in such a way as to make God's will clear. In such cases, the guidance is so obvious that to refuse it would be the same as disobedience (Acts 11:12; 16:6, 7).

One further word—when God gives light, walk in it (Acts 26:19). Guidance must be obeyed to be continued. Obedience is the basis of a life of true happiness and lasting value.

Chapter 21

PRAYER AND PRAISE

WHAT DOES THE BIBLE TEACH about prayer? There can be no progress in any part of the Christian life without prayer. It is therefore important for the young believer to know what the Bible teaches about this subject. The following outline is intended to answer some basic questions:

1. *Why pray?* Because the Bible commands us to do so (I Timothy 2:8). The Lord Jesus was a man of prayer. If He felt the need of it, how much more should we! (I Thessalonians 5:17, 18; Ephesians 6:18).

2. *How often?* We should pray at set times each day, and then, in between those times. It is a good plan to pray upon arising in the morning and upon retiring at night. Then during the day, we should look to the Lord when problems arise,

when help is needed or when we want to thank Him for something. Certainly every Christian should bow his head and give thanks before eating his meals, whether in public or at home.

3. *In what position?* Daniel kneeled when he prayed (Daniel 6:10). So did the Lord Jesus (Luke 22:41). Nehemiah, on the other hand, prayed while he was standing before the king (Nehemiah 2:4). In general, Christians kneel when at home, but it is still their privilege to speak to God while walking along the street or engaging in their daily activities.

4. *For what?* Among the Scriptures which answer this question are Philippians 4:6; I Timothy 2:1-3; and Matthew 9:38. There is nothing too small and nothing too great for prayer. Many believers find it helpful to keep a prayer list on which they record such items as:

(a) names of unsaved relatives and friends.

(b) names of those who are sick or in need.

(c) names of those who are serving the Lord, such as missionaries, evangelists, teachers, etc.

Where your requests are specific, you will see specific answers; whereas, if you pray for people in general, without naming them, you will have no way of knowing whether your prayers are answered.

5. *Conditions for answered prayer?*

(a) If we abide in Christ, our requests will be answered (John 15:7). Abiding in Christ means keeping His commandments (I John 3:22).

(b) Our prayers should be according to His will (I John 5:14). Since the general outline of God's will is found in the Bible, our requests should be Scriptural. Therefore, pray in the language of the Bible.

(c) Our requests should be offered in the Name of Christ (John 14:13; 16:23). When we truly ask in His Name, it is the same as if He were making the request of God.

(d) Our motives must be pure (James 4:3). If our motives are selfish and sinful, we cannot expect an answer.

6. *Language of prayer?* We should address God reverently. Christians commonly use the words "Thou" and "Thee" instead of the more familiar "You" in speaking to their Father.

7. *Dangers of prayer.*

(a) Don't pray to be seen (Matthew 6:5, 6).

(b) Don't ask God to do something you can do yourself. No sane Christian would step into the path of an oncoming auto and then ask God to take him back to the sidewalk. God gave him legs to take himself back.

(c) Don't ask for something you know you shouldn't have! God *sometimes* grants such requests but sends leanness to the soul (Psalm 106:15).

(d) Avoid meaningless repetitions (Matthew 6:7; Ecclesiastes 5:2).

8. *Other suggestions.*

(a) If you find that your mind wanders when you are on your knees, try praying out loud. This will greatly help you to concentrate.

(b) Don't be discouraged if your answer does not come immediately. God's answers are never too early lest we miss the blessedness of waiting upon Him, and never too late lest we think that we have trusted Him in vain.

(c) If God's answer is not exactly what you asked for, remember this: God reserves the right to give us something better than we ask for. We do not know what is best for us, but He does, and so He gives us more than we could ever ask or think (II Corinthians 12:8, 9).

Chapter 22

WITNESSING AND WINNING

HOW CAN A CHRISTIAN lead others to Christ? Winning souls to Jesus Christ is one of the greatest occupations in the world today (Proverbs 11:30). Although there are no hard and fast rules to insure success in this work, yet there are some general principles which will prove extremely valuable.

1. It is of first importance that the soul-winner himself be spiritually healthy. He must be constantly feeding on the Word. He must spend much time in prayer. He must be yielded to God. He must confess and abandon any cherished sins. By thus walking in the Spirit, the Christian will find that the Lord will provide opportunities for effectual witness. This is undoubtedly the Golden Rule of soul-winning—"Live close to God" (Matthew 4:19).

2. It is a good thing to start each day by asking God to lead us to those whom He wants us to contact. It is obvious that we cannot speak to everyone we see. It is also clear that we have no way of knowing by ourselves which souls are "ripe" for salvation. But if we let the Lord lead us, we will work more efficiently, and reap more fruit for Him.

3. Then during the day we should seize the opportunities to speak for Christ. When fellow-workers use the Name of the Lord in profanity, for instance, there is often opportunity for a tactful, loving word of testimony. Religious subjects often come up in conversation; we should make the most of them. Then again we do not always have to wait for opportunities: we can make them for ourselves. Worldly men talk freely about politics, the weather and sports. Why should our lips be sealed about Christ, our Redeemer?

4. Quote the Word of God as much as possible. It is a living Word! (Hebrews 4:12). It has power to reach souls far beyond any words we could ever utter. It is the Sword of the Spirit, and every good soldier of Jesus Christ should use this greatest of all weapons. Unsaved men will do everything in their power to stop you from recit-

ing Scripture verses. But don't stop. If they say that they don't believe the Bible, quote more of it.

5. Follow up each contact. Not many persons are saved the first time they hear the Gospel. Usually they have to be spoken to again and again. Show little kindnesses to them. Hand them good Gospel literature. Invite them to attend Gospel meetings with you. Above all, be much in prayer for them. Do not be discouraged if some are hostile to you. Opposition is often a sign that they are being convicted by the Holy Spirit, whereas indifference is almost impossible to deal with.

6. Don't press for quick decisions. A false profession is not only worthless, but it may deceive the individual himself, and may do untold harm to the cause of Christ. You be faithful in sowing the seed, and God will be faithful in giving the increase.

7. If you find it difficult to speak to others about the Lord, tell the Lord about it and ask Him to give you strength and courage to witness for Him. If you really want it, He will give it.

8. Always carry a good supply of Gospel literature with you. You can not only pass tracts to those you meet, but can leave them on street cars or busses, in restaurants, or almost any public place.

The rewards of soul-winning are tremendous.

1. The present joys of leading a person to Christ are indescribable! (Luke 15:10).

2. How much greater will be the joy in heaven when someone greets you with these words, "It was you who invited me here!"

3. Finally, how incomparable will be the thrill when the Lord Jesus Christ openly confesses you before the assembled hosts of heaven (Matthew 10:32).

In view of this, let our constant prayer be:

Let me look on the crowd as my Savior did,
Till my eyes with tears grow dim;
Let me view with pity the wandering sheep,
And love them for love of Him (Matthew 9:36).

Chapter 23

SEARCHING THE SCRIPTURES

WHAT SHOULD A CHRISTIAN know about Bible study? Bible study must be carried on in full dependence on the Holy Spirit. He is our teacher, and we should constantly seek His guidance (John 14:26; 16:13).

There is no quick, easy way to learn the Bible. It involves hard work for everyone. Yet it is also true that the more knowledge of it we gain, the easier it is to gain additional knowledge.

The Bible student should first of all have tools to work with:

1. *A good study Bible.* The Scofield Reference Bible is excellent. The text is the same as the regular King James or Authorized version, but helpful notes are added to explain difficult passages.

2. *A good concordance.* This enables you to find a verse when you can remember only a word

or two in it. The three best concordances are Strong's, Young's and Cruden's. The first two are more complete, but the last is less costly and gives the English words only. (The former give the Greek and Hebrew.)

3. A *good Bible dictionary*. This contains a wealth of information on Bible subjects. Smith's or Peloubet's is satisfactory for the beginner.

Having provided himself with the necessary equipment, the believer is ready to embark on a serious study of the Scriptures.

1. The first thing to do is set aside a definite time each day, and begin reading the Bible. It is a good plan to start at Matthew and go through the New Testament. Then begin at Genesis and read through the entire Bible. Don't read so that you can say you've been through the Bible, but read so you will know what the Bible says.

2. When you come to an unfamiliar word, look it up in the Bible dictionary or in a regular dictionary. If you come to a passage you cannot understand, first try to get the meaning by studying it carefully. If this fails, make a note of the problem, and look it up in a Bible commentary when you get a chance. Among the helpful commentar-

ies are those by Matthew Henry, and Jamieson, Faussett and Brown.

3. Compare Scripture with Scripture. Don't try to build a doctrine on a single verse. Find out what is the consistent teaching in all the Bible on the subject. "Truth does not contradict truth."

4. You will be well rewarded if you write down an outline of each chapter, answering the following questions:

(a) What have I learned about Christ? (Even in the Old Testament you will find the Savior in types and shadows.)

(b) What is the principal message of this chapter?

(c) What precious promise may I claim?

(d) Which is the outstanding verse?

(e) What sin am I taught to avoid?

(f) What example is there for me to follow?

(g) What are the difficult verses?

5. During the day you should try to discuss what you have read with someone else. This will serve two purposes: it will help to fix the lesson in your own mind; it will enable someone else to share the blessing which you received from your Bible study (Malachi 3:16).

6. Try to memorize two or three verses of

Scripture each week. Begin with familiar Gospel verses such as: John 1:12; John 3:16; John 3:36; John 5:24; Romans 10:9, etc. Review all memory verses constantly until you really *have* them. You will find your own life enriched, and you will be better able to speak to others.

7. The great goal of Bible study, of course, is to put into practice what you have learned. We should allow the Word to rebuke us, to correct us, to make us more like the Lord Jesus (Jeremiah 15:16).

Remember when you study the Bible you are studying an eternal book. Everything you learn about it here is an investment for eternity. So give it your very best.

Chapter 24

THE LIFE THAT COUNTS

HOW CAN A CHRISTIAN make his life count? Although a believer cannot lose his salvation, it is certainly true that he can waste his life so that it will not count for eternity. It has been rightly said, "A fool is a man all of whose plans end in time." To avoid the tragedy of a wasted life, the Bible counsels every Christian as follows:

1. Count the cost of being a disciple of Christ. All believers are children of God, but not all are disciples. The terms of discipleship are given in Matthew 10:16-42 and Luke 14:25-35. To be a disciple means giving up comforts and earthly security. It means a life of self-denial. It means the enmity and ridicule of the world. It means forsaking all to follow the Lord Jesus.

2. Make a deliberate commitment of your life to Him (Romans 12:1). Come to that point of de-

cision where you yield your body a living sacrifice to God. This is the only reasonable thing to do in view of all that He has done. C. T. Studd once said, "If Jesus Christ is God and died for me, then no sacrifice can be too great for me to make for Him."

3. Abandon your life for Christ. The Savior said, "Whosoever will lose his life for my sake shall find it" (Matthew 16:25). In other words, if you want to know the full joy and happiness of life, you should live to please the Lord Jesus Christ and not yourself. The one who lives selfishly is a miserable, unhappy person.

4. Burn your bridges behind you. "Bind the sacrifice with cords, even unto the horns of the altar" (Psalm 118:27). Make it as difficult as possible for yourself to turn back by severing all connections that would keep you from a life of wholehearted obedience and devotion to your Lord (Luke 9:23).

5. Don't be sidetracked. So many start off well but then they lose the vision and slip back into the old routine. Good paying jobs divert many. Interesting careers lure others away. Unwise marriages have been the downfall of many a would-be disciple. The Lord Jesus said, "No man, having

put his hand to the plow, and looking back, is fit for the kingdom of God" (Luke 9:62).

6. Live to serve. "The Son of Man came not to be ministered unto, but to minister" (Matthew 20:28). True greatness lies in serving others. Don't try to be on the receiving line. "It is more blessed to give than to receive" (Acts 20:35).

7. Crown Him Lord of all. If Christ rules in your life, your days will really count for eternity.

At the close of this Bible course, we should like to impress on the student that Christianity is "not a pleasant pastime but a passionate quest." It is not an easy life but a struggle. It costs nothing to become a Christian but it costs everything to be one. It is not popularity but persecution; not comfort but a cross.

But it is the best life. You serve the best of Masters. Your wages are good, but you like your work even better than your wages. Your rewards are wonderful, both now and in eternity.

We urge you, therefore, to give your life to Christ. Give Him your very best. Hold nothing back. May it be your supreme joy to hear Him say to you at last, "Well done, thou good and faithful servant . . . enter thou into the joy of thy Lord" (Matthew 25:21).